THE BLUE HEN
by Des Dillon

Greenend was rough – the roughest scheme in Coatbridge. John and me thought it couldn't get any rougher. We were wrong. The closing down of the steelworks meant the end of being in work – but John and his pal don't intend it to be the end of keeping afloat. Keep hens – that's the answer. Or become window cleaners? But it's harder than you'd think to be the only honest guys in a place like Greenend.

Des Dillon is an award winning poet, short story writer, novelist and dramatist for film, television and stage. Born and brought up in Coatbridge, Lanarkshire, he was Writer in Residence in Castlemilk, Glasgow 1998–2000. He was TAPS Writer of The Year 2000, and won an SAC Writers' Award in the same year. On World Book Day 2003 his novel *Me and Ma Gal* was voted the book that best evokes contemporary Scotland. He lives in Galloway.

D1354152

By the same author.

Fiction
Me and ma Gal
The Big Empty
Duck
Itchycooblue
Return of the Busby Babes
The Big Q
Six Black Candles

Poetry
Sniz
Palacerigg
Picking Brambles

Drama
Six Black Candles
The Bay
Lockerbie 103

THE BLUE HEN

Des Dillon

SANDSTONE vista 2

The Sandstone Vista Series

The Blue Hen by Des Dillon
First published 2004 in Great Britain by Sandstone Press Ltd
PO Box 5725, Dingwall, Ross-shire, IV15 9WJ, Scotland

The publisher acknowledges the financial assistance of the
Literacies Initiative of the Highland Community Learning
Strategy Partnership.

ISBN 0-9546333-0-X

The Sandstone Vista Series of novellas has
been written and skilfully edited
for the enjoyment of readers with differing levels
of reading skills, from the emergent to the accomplished.

Designed and typeset by Edward Garden Graphic Design,
Dingwall, Ross-shire, Scotland.

Printed and bound by Dingwall Printers Ltd,
Dingwall, Ross-shire, Scotland.

www.sandstonepress.com

This book is dedicated to my two brothers
Stevie and David.

CHAPTER ONE

Greenend was all four-in-a-block houses. In the late seventies it was rough. The roughest scheme in Coatbridge. Me and John up the stairs thought it couldn't get any rougher. We were wrong.

Me and John shared a garden. We kept it in good nick. Planted tatties and radishes and tomatoes. Every night we'd come home from the Klondike and do a couple of hours before we got washed up. The whole scheme worked in the Klondike. Made steel tubes for gas pipelines and giant steel rolls for the car industry. Big Bannan worked there too and even though he done a bit of money-lending, he was an alright guy.

'Never had a bad bone in his body back then,' John said. That was going to change. Big style.

I mind the time Bannan brung in six eggs and we fried them on a Motherwell-Number-Nine shovel heated up in the furnace. We flung them on rolls and scoffed them with a can of Carlsberg Special each. They were the days. Life was good. Life was two rolls on egg. Life was the snow melting on the black corrugated roof of the Klondike and us three slugging lager.

'It doesn't get any better than this,' Bannen said.

After work on a Friday we didn't go home to the garden. We went down to the Wire Inn for a few jars. John's Maw worked there as a cleaner. And at night she was a barmaid. Alright, she wasn't the best looking barmaid in the world but she slipped me, John and Bannan the odd glass of Eldorado and sometimes even a wee goldie.

'Away you up and get yourself washed,' she'd say to John every time we got our drinks.

'Aye! Aye!' he'd go.

We'd usually leave about eleven. But sometimes we'd get a 'lock in'. Drink in the pub till dawn. We were never short of money. If you ran out midweek you'd tap Bannan for ten or twenty and pay him back on the Friday. He only took a pound in the tenner. That was going to change big style too. Cos Thatcher came in and started closing down works everywhere. Everybody knew it was only a matter of time for the Klondike. To be honest I thought it would be quite good. No work. Pottering about all day in the garden. Going for walks. Maybe take up a hobby. I was even looking forward to getting a Giro. If I was careful and drank less I'd be able to go to the Wire Inn on a Friday and Saturday. A Sunday too if John's Maw could slip us more drinks than usual.

It was the early eighties when we heard they were shutting the Klondike. I asked John about it. I expected him to be happy but he wasn't.

'It'll be great, John,' I goes. 'Us in the garden all day. All the things we could grow. Maybe even sell.'

But no matter how I tried I couldn't cheer him up.

That night the whole work was in the Wire Inn drinking. Laughing. It was a right good crack. They had got a karaoke machine and 'My Way' was a favourite. 'And now the end is near'. Everybody was up singing. Except John. I got him in the wee corner where the old men usually play dominoes and asked him what was up.

'Are you worried about not having a job?'

'It's not me not having a job I'm worried about,' he said, 'it's the whole scheme not having a job.'

We sat in the corner the rest of the night watching all the men enjoying their selves. There were times that night when I thought John was going to cry. He's deep as the deep blue sea, so he is. He was looking ahead. He could see Greenend's future. About half-ten I was coming back from the bar with more drinks and he was staring at the floor. I felt sorry for him. I put the drinks on the table and ruffled his hair.

'You're as deep as the deep blue sea, John,' I said. And that seemed to cheer him up a bit cos when I sat down he put his arm round me and slapped my back.

'You'll be alright,' he said, 'you'll be fine.'

But he said it like everybody else was damned. Except for me and him. Then he leaned forward and kissed me on the forehead.

CHAPTER TWO

So the Klondike shut down. It's like it was yesterday. The last day. I remember walking out and leaving the echo of my boots inside. Like I'd left my ghost behind. And at night the big dark building looked haunted. It was the first time it had been quiet in a hundred years. Me and John snuck in sometimes when the security guards were sleeping. We'd walk about sharing a bottle of Buckie. Every noise was dead loud. Even our breathing. You had to put your feet down careful and speak only in whispers.

This night a big seagull flew in. It sounded like a flock of angels trapped in hell as it flapped across the Klondike – terrified. Looking for a way out. Me and John crouched in a corner and watched. It would fly round the edge of the giant building screaming then stop exhausted on a steel beam. Opening and shutting its big yellow beak. Then it would take off again looking. After an hour John couldn't take any more and opened one of the big skylights. The seagull smelled the fresh air and whooshed out. Soaring up into the sky. And there was silence. John started crying.

'What's wrong, John?' I said.

'It's hard to believe all the good times we had in here are gone. Forever.'

I was going to tell him they weren't gone. They were in here. In our heads. But the security guards must've heard the skylight opening. They were coming down the work swinging their torch beams about. Me and John snuck away.

The Klondike shut in the November and Greenend partied right through Christmas. Right into the New Year. Everybody thought their redundancy money would last forever. But by March it was all gone. The party was over. It was only Bannan who had money. And now he was taking three quid in the tenner.

The Klondike stood on the edge of the scheme like a huge black ship lost at sea. A giant black hulk in an ocean of white snow. Then, one day, somebody noticed the security guards were gone.

The Klondike was there for the picking. That night the whole scheme descended on it and stripped every bit of scrap metal. Cast iron, lead, copper, aluminium and platinum. Bannan's gang got the silver from the electric switchgear. Greenend had another party. Then the money ran out again.

Some of the corner boys had found a way to melt aluminium beer barrels. You get an oil drum, knock holes in the sides, and light a good fire in it. Once it's going like a wee furnace you sit the beer barrel inside and it melts down into a big snottery ingot. Then you can sell them to scrap metal merchants. They don't take beer barrels. But that only lasted a few weeks. The Wire Inn got wise and started keeping all the beer barrels inside. By the beginning of April there was nothing. Again.

The year was balanced between winter and spring. Everything was grey. The pavements. People's faces. The buildings. The sky. The future. Nobody in the scheme had a job. Not one solitary single soul. Even John's Maw had been paid off from the Wire Inn. Not enough punters. Men whose money had ran out were gathering on the corner. They'd be passing Buckie and dope. Trying to numb their selves. Me and John never took the dope when they passed it to us. It was just the drink we liked. Before the Klondike shut down drugs were only for hippies and weirdos. But now unemployed moulders and turners and puddlers and labourers were tugging away at joints. You'd think it couldn't get any worse. But it did.

Smack came onto the scene. Bannan took to drug-dealing like a duck. It seemed like one week he was outside the Post Office collecting his Money Lending Payments from people cashing their Monday Books. The next week he had a big Japanese four-wheel drive. A Shogun it was called. I said to John there must be good money in drugs.

'There's always money in misery,' John said.

CHAPTER THREE

A year later there's a junkie in nearly every close. Even the houses look depressed. There's steel shutters on windows all over the scheme cos of the people that have flitted away. The more smack Bannan sells, the more things change. You were starting to get junkies shooting up outside. I goes up for John this night. I had a bottle of Buckie up my jook. I was thinking about the first slug burning its way down my gullet. Hitting my belly like a mother's love.

I chaps John's door and he peeks out the letterbox. I push the Buckie bottle up till the golden cork's poking out my jumper.

'Coming down the corner?' I says.

But John wasn't going down the corner that night. Or the next night. Or any other night.

'The corner's stepped over the line,' he said.

'There's no way back now.'

I could see what he was saying. Needles were on the corner. A wean got jagged by one and had to get blood tests. And last week Bannan stabbed a welder from the Whifflet trying to move in on his patch. He's in the Monklands. Critical. The polis came but nobody would say anything. They took Bannan in but that night he was back on the corner in his big silver Shogun laughing and giving out orders.

If John's not happy with the corner – I'm not happy with the corner. So, even though his Maw doesn't like it, we sat in his scullery drinking. Talking about the corner. John says there's corners all over the country like it. Men gathered up. And it's like when they gassed the Jews he said. Only it's not bodies that's piled up and destroyed but souls. People's spirit.

'By the turn of the century the whole country'll pay for it. Mark my words,' he said.

It was making him angry so I asked what about the garden? 'What's our plans?' He looked out over the garden. Thinking.

Then he turns and says, 'Things're tight and they're not going to get any better. If you want to at least keep your dignity you've got to have goals. Long term plans.'

We thought about plans. But came up with nothing. John started to get depressed. So I starts talking about good times in the Klondike. Frying eggs on shovels. Drinking lager. Having a laugh.

'They were some days John eh? The best time of our lives! Eh John?'

He looked at me. At first I couldn't make out the look. Then I realized it was hope. Hope for the first time since the Klondike shut. It was the eggs that done it.

John thought we should get chickens. It was a great idea. I took a swig and handed him the bottle by way of a toast. We figured we could get six or even a dozen eggs a day. That with the carrots and radishes and spuds we were already growing could save us a fortune. Soft boiled eggs and omelettes were lighting up in my head.

Next day we went round the Whifflet library and looked up chickens and eggs and hutches. The hutch was easy enough to build. We got the wood from the swing-park fence. Bannan's Maw was looking out her back window wondering what the sawing was and – hey! Off walks an eight feet section of council fence. We never thought we were doing any damage cos the swing park had no swings. Just some broke slabs and a universe of smashed glass shrapnel. Sometimes on a clear night if you stared into the bits of glass you'd see starlight in them. You never knew if you were looking at the heaven or earth.

A week later and four eight feet lengths of fencing – we've built a chicken run. In the book it says to hang a hundred watt bulb inside so the chicks can huddle round it. I ran the wire from my house cos I had my Powercard meter wired up to run for nothing anyway. John took the bulb out his back room that they never used except if they got visitors. All we needed now was the chicks.

We went down across the M8 to Bankhead Farm where they were doing chicks for fifty pence each. Twenty we bought. A tenner. And that was a lot of money to us. We'd been saving it up out of our Giros for weeks. We put the chicks in the run and watched. They were like wee yellow cartoon characters buzzing about. Searching and pecking and sniffing in their new home. But they're not as daft as they look, chicks. Soon they were all piling over each other to get below the hundred watt bulb. The cheeping and the smell of sawdust and all them chicks squeezing into the light made me feel good. A wee yellow ball of life. Me and John smiled at each other. It was a great feeling and we both looked forward to omelettes and soft boiled eggs. I know that because we talked about it all the time. We couldn't go five minutes without one of us bringing up omelettes and eggs. Eggs and omelettes. All we had to do now was feed them and watch them grow.

At night I'd sit at my window looking at the slither of warm light beaming across the garden. I'd imagine the quiet burble of the chicks pressing round the bulb. Snoring maybe. If that's what they do. And then, now and then, one of them falls out the bundle and scutters round the other side and launches itself into the pile. Looking for a place nearer to the heat of the great bulb sun God.

The spuds and the other stuff were doing fine in the garden. We'd even took up some radishes and made pieces on margarine with a bit of salt. I love the way they crunch when your teeth arrive through the soft bread – mm!

Well – the chicks soon passed that wee lovely stage and turned into these pre-historic monsters. Their crazed gaze said they'd tear the eye out your head if you gave them half the chance. Sometimes if John wasn't there and they were all staring at me I'd get a bit scared and have to shut the lid. But if he was there I'd not mention it and try to see if I could see it in his eyes. You can't mention fear in Greenend.

On and on it went and they got bigger and uglier. Then one morning I went out and there was one lying dead. I chipped a few stones up at John's and out he came with his Maw's slippers squeezed onto his feet and her housecoat wrapped round him. We held it up by the claw and looked at the white slither of death over the ball of its eye. We were really worried that it could be some chicken disease. That we'd lose the whole lot.

CHAPTER FOUR

In the library there wasn't much about chicken diseases. It was mostly all good news about chickens. How to get the best eggs and stuff. We told ourselves it must've died of natural causes. On the way home we rubbed out one soft boiled egg each from the future menu in our heads.

But when we got home and lifted the lid there was another one dead. Eye pecked out. Bloodied stalks hanging out the socket like fibre-optics. John checked a few of the chicks and found marks here and there. Scars.

So that's it. Fights. These chicks were now teenagers. When we looked about to see who was responsible every eye was evil. Every eye intense. Like when I got my telly knocked. Smack was just taking its grip and for the first time in Greenend, houses were getting broke into. Every

Junkie grinning on the corner the next day – I thought it was him. It's not easy to spot evil.

I said we should separate the chicks into two groups and see what group's got a dead one the next day. Narrow it down till we find the killer. The psycho chicken. But John made an intelligent point.

'What if they're all killers?' he says.

And there's no getting by that. If they're all killers we'd need to put them in solitary confinement. We'd need to build a massive hutch for that and I don't think the burgh fence could take another hit. We went to bed that night a bit subdued but took the curse off it with a bottle of Buckfast between us.

Since we got made redundant, John hardly ever got out his bed before twelve. But I wasn't surprised to meet him in the close at half-nine the next morning. He'd been up all night same as me. Worrying about the chicks. We went out into the garden.

We opened the lid together. Looked. Two dead. The rest were chattering on the corner like Bannan and his mob. John shakes his head and leaves me to close the lid. He walks to the other end of the garden and kicks this old shed. He puts a hole right through it in fact. But that's nothing cos it's all rotted away. Just like this whole place. And he never says much John but when he does it makes a difference.

'Men don't lay eggs!'

'What?' I goes.

'Men don't lay eggs,' he says with his palms firing out the meaning. I get it. I go and have a boot at the old shed myself. He's right. We bought all them chicks but we never checked to see what ones were hens. For all we know it's all cockerels we've got.

What to do? Back to the library. The book wasn't much help. Back home. We looked for dicks and stuff between their big rubbery claws. But there was nothing to see. Then John came up with a great idea. His best yet. He's a bit of a psychologist John so he is.

'What applies to human beings applies just as well to chickens. The ones that've already died are probably male. All this territorial shite that goes on down the corner. Like Bannan and his drug-dealing. The cockerels are probably killing each other for control of the hens. It's a sex thing.

Great!' he says.

And I give him a 'how's that great?' look when he explains it to me.

'Well, how many of the corner team d'you know that attack lassies?'

'None!'

'Exactly. So if we let things take their course we'll be left with one male and the rest'll be hens!'

That makes a lot of sense. For the first time in ages the whole thing takes on a happy glow. And something else John says too.

'The male that's left – that'll be the Bannan of the chicken run. If we start a breeding programme we'll have the best genes in the pool.'

Christ! Things were getting better by the minute. Half of me wanted the weak chickens to be dead already.

But by the end of June the happiness of that day had faded. There was only one chicken left. And it was a big Rhode Island Red. A Rooster. Me and John couldn't believe how unlucky we'd been. We'd bought twenty chickens and they all turned out to be male. The very last omelette went pop in both our heads at the same time. You'd think things couldn't get any worse.

But they did.

The Red Rooster started cock-a-doodle-dooing at four in the morning. There was nothing you could do. People were starting to make comments. Not bad stuff – 'Is that your chicken I heard this morning?' Stuff like that. I talked to John about it but he seemed to have gave up. I knew he'd finally let go when the bulb went on the blink. Even though my electricity was stole it was still me that was providing it for the chicken hutch. I felt it was morally right that John should provide the bulb. When I asked him he never said no. He just said that his Maw had asked where the bulb was in the visitors' bedroom and he'd to go and nick one out the Doctor's. I looked at him. He looked back. There was no bulb coming out of him, so I used the one out my toilet. But I was feeling a bit resentful at the whole thing by now. And it's hard to shake off a resentment when you're getting woke up at four every morning by a big Red Rooster.

I decided not to fall out with John. So we chewed the fat as if the chickens had never happened. And we carried on drinking in his

scullery cos by now the corner was a no go area.
The Red Rooster ruled the garden.

CHAPTER FIVE

John still had plans for the future. There was no way he was going to end up on the corner. And he said he was going to make sure I didn't end up on the corner either. I never seen him for a couple of weeks. Then he taps on my window this morning about six. He took me out the back and there was this great aluminium ladder. I asked him where he got it. They'd started knocking the Klondike down and he stole it. And that's not all he's got.

'Taa naa!' he says and produces two buckets and cloths. He got them out his Maw's cleaning press.

We started a window cleaning run in Greenend. Not many people could waste money on getting their windows cleaned. But we were only charging fifty pence a house. I know it's not much but it made us a few bob for drink. We'd do half the scheme one week and the other half the next week. That usually made us forty quid. Twenty each. Not bad on top of the Giro. When we passed Bannan and his gang they'd shout abuse at us. Once Bannan tried to take the ladder off John. But John was a stoker on the furnaces and all that shovelling gives you some grip. They stood with the ladder across the road. Bannan at one end and John at the other. Tugging. The traffic had built up at each end. Bannan pulled but I could have told him there was no way John was letting go. John would never give up. Bannan pulled out a knife and flung it to one of his henchmen. It was McKinney. McKinney comes at John. I had to do something. I stood in front of John. When McKinney moved left, I moved left. When he moved right, I moved right.

'Out the road,' says McKinney. I didn't say nothing. I just stood there.

'Slash him and all!' Bannan shouted.

But the polis had drew up to see what the traffic jam was all about. McKinney lobbed the knife into a garden and walked away. Bannan let go of the ladder and the cars got going. Me and John walked away carrying the ladder.

When we got to the other end of the street the polis stopped. It was Butsy Riley. John was at school with him.

'Everything alright John?'

'Aye Butsy.'

'He's getting too big for his boots,' says Butsy about Bannan and drove off.

We kept out Bannan's way and carried on cleaning windows. By August we had built up a lot of customers. We were quite good at the windows. All the women were satisfied with our work. The chickens were well forgot except for the Red Rooster waking us up in the mornings.

Sometimes in life everything happens at once. This is one of them times. We went along to start the windows about eight one morning. We kept the ladders under Skib Martin's garage in Southfield Crescent. Nobody had ever touched them before so we never expected them to be gone. There used to be a rule that you never interfere with a workman's tools. That's how he puts the bread on the table. That was something else that had changed.

You could see the ladders were missing from the pavement but John went up anyway and I followed him. John took his anger out on Skib's garage. He booted it a couple of times and so did I. I was doing it more in comradeship than anger. But John set about it again. He was tearing lumps of wood off it and flinging them across the gardens. Skib came out. He was the original hard man. He had fists on him like car batteries. In his day there was no man could beat him. That was in the days when you were a coward if you used a knife. He was John's Da's pal. He was there when John's Da got melted in the Klondike. They were pouring a hundred tons of molten steel into a giant roll. But it was water cooled. It leaked and it exploded, evaporated five men. Skib tried to save John's Da. He still had the burn marks on his hands and face.

'What's your game John?' says Skib and gets hold of John. He held him against the garage till his temper died. Me and John told Skib about our window cleaning run and how the ladder got stole.

'Stole?' says Skib. 'Bannan came and got it yesterday. Said yous said it was okay!'

John was crying. He apologised to Skib and walked away. I mind the look in Skib's eye as he watched John walk to the gate. He shouted and John turned back.

'Your Da would've been proud of you son. Keep it up.'

Me and John walked away. John in total silence. Skib knew John was trying to live a decent life. That's what he meant when he said his Da would be proud of him.

When I thought John was calm enough to talk I showed him the twenty I had in my tail. I got a wee Giro through. Sometime you'd get a surprise Giro cos they were paying you short for a while. It was always good to get one of them. We went to the carry out shop. By half one we were steaming. I don't know how we got there but we ended up across from the corner. John was staring at Bannan sitting smoking in his Shogun.

'Haw Bannan!' John shouted.

Bannan turned and grinned.

'How's the windy cleaning run going?' he shouted and laughed.

John lost it. He ran over and started kicking the panels in on Bannan's car. I was trying to pull him away. Bannan never done nothing. He just kept on saying Ooh. Ouch and all that. Like it was him

John was kicking. His men done nothing. I expected me and John to get a right doing. But they stood looking at us. That's when I noticed two polis. It was Butsy and the other one with red hair. They pulled John back. They don't want to lift anybody. It's a nice day and they probably want to drive about ignoring junkies and winos and get their shift in. But John's got other ideas. He puts the boot into the door panel again.

'Right, that's it,' says Bannan to Butsy. 'I want him lifted!'

The polis have got no option but to lift John. I remember John's face disappearing in the back window of the polis car. When the car turned left at the roundabout Bannan's gang chased me. But I'm quite a fast runner and I was in the middle of the scheme in jig time. Hiding behind some hedges. I still had a bottle of Buckie so I went up the swing park and drank that. But it wasn't the same without John.

CHAPTER SIX

I woke up on the slabs where the swings used to be. I was freezing. It came back to me about John getting huckled. It was still early so I went up and waited on him coming out the cells at six. They always let you out at six if you're just drunk. The only thing John was worried about was that he'd be in the Advertiser and his Maw would see it. But I got him onto the subject of ladders. It was only a matter of time before some other window cleaner moved in and took our patch. There's nothing you can do unless you want a window cleaning war. John didn't seem to care. All he wanted to do was go home to his bed. When we got to the close the Red Rooster was up on the gutter watching us. It made a couple of clucks, turned and walked up the slates. Perching itself on the apex of the roof.

By Wednesday me and John had forgot all about him getting lifted. But the Advertiser came out and he was in it. A man was arrested in Greenend at the weekend after an incident with a passing motorist. It had John's name in it. He came down to my house and flapped it on the table.

'My Maw's going mental,' he says. 'Threatened to chuck me out.'

We didn't have any money for drink so I made us tea and we sat watching the Red Rooster strut about the garden peck pecking at the ground. After a while depression fell over John's face like a shroud and he said he was away up the stairs for a sleep. He was tired. I knew I wouldn't be seeing him for a while.

Don't you worry John, I said to myself, I'll get a pair of ladders and keep the run going. I didn't like to see him depressed. I signed on the B'roo on a Wednesday so on the way home I kept my eyes peeled for ladders. But ladders are like buses. You can never get them when you want them. When I got home I looked up and the Venetian blinds in John's room were shut. That was a bad sign.

I woke up on Friday morning with this feeling that time was running out. The women in Greenend were expecting their windows to be cleaned. If me and John didn't get our act together theyd just give the nod to some other window cleaner and he'd take over. My Giro arrived and I was tempted to buy a carry-out and take it up to John's. But when he was depressed he never wanted to see nobody.

I got a bottle of Buckie and two cans and sat on the kerb trying to figure the situation out. Everybody that goes by I ask them if they've got any ladders they can lend me. They all seen a pair somewhere but can't remember exactly where. By the time I'm ready for another bottle I'm stumped as far as ladders go.

That night, I'm lying on my couch and – Bing! It comes to me. Jim Kerr's got a wee mark one Cortina C-reg. It's always round his back and he never uses it. You can start it with a screwdriver. Everybody steals it now and then. They always take it back. Usually with petrol in it. That's cos they like Jim. They like him cos he tells great lies. He's been round the world twice without leaving his room. It's got a roof rack.

When I get there somebody's left a screwdriver on the dash. That's handy. I jump in and starts her up. I've got two bottles of Buckie and six tins to keep me going. All night long I'm prowling the streets in this Cortina looking for ladders. Every place you think there's bound to be a pair – there's none. There was new houses going up everywhere. It was a strange time. Here we were in Greenend poverty stricken and just over the canal they were building houses that cost seventy-odd grand. Something was wrong but I've not got the brains to work it out. They had two security guards and a big dog on that site. When they pulled me up I said I was lost and drove away. The dog barked till it couldn't see me anymore.

I went to what was left of the Klondike. They'd nearly finished knocking it down. It was all bulldozers and metal huts. No ladders. I searched all the closed down steelworks. Nothing. Tried the painter and decorators. Nope. The British Telecom base. Not a rung and I'm getting drunker by the minute. By the middle of the night I'm that drunk I've got to hold one hand over my eye to see right. There's two of everything. I decide to get an hour's kip. See if that'll sober me up.

When I wake up it's dawn and still there's no ladders. The car's low on petrol and I've got to take it back to Jim Kerr's. I turn into his street and I think I'm seeing things with the drink. There's a big shiny pair of aluminium ladders propped up against the wall. Like God's felt sorry for me and left them there.

I get them on the roof rack. Tie them on with a couple of jumpers off a washing line and drive off. I can't wait for John to see the new ladders. I decide to go right now. As I'm driving up tears start sniffling down my face. You know what it's like when you're drunk. I start to feel like some comic book hero. Saving the day by getting my pal the ladders he needs to keep his business going. I felt really good. Like I was doing something that made a difference. It didn't feel like stealing at all. Committing a sin. Thou shalt not steal big pair of ladders to keep your window cleaning run going so that your pal John can come out of his depression.

By the time I got to John's I was a bubbling wreck. This thought comes into my head. I get the ladders up at John's room window. I've got a half finished bottle of Buckie in one hand and I'm rat-a-tat-tatting at the window with the other. It's only half five in the morning. I can hear John sitting up in bed inside and listening. Like he's been dreaming and he's not sure if there's somebody at the window.

He's sure I'm real when I pull the window open and crash in through the Venetian blinds. I bump onto the floor with the blinds wrapped round me like a crazy hula dancer. My body is poking up through the sea of slats. It's just the top half of my body and a bottle of Buckie. John's head is pressed back against the headboard.

I hold the bottle up in the air.

'Taa naa!' I say, 'We're back in business. I've got ladders.'

Me and John got drunk that day and went back into the window cleaning next morning. John was cheered right up. I had been feeding and taking care of the Red Rooster since he washed his hands of the whole chicken situation. He'd never ever mentioned it. But this day when we were cleaning windows in Southfield Crescent he asked how the Red Rooster was doing and chatted away good style. He even laughed at how daft we were, thinking we'd bought hens and they'd all been roosters. Everything was going fine. It looked like John's depression was away.

Then Bannan stole the ladders again. We kept them in our back garden this time. But John's Maw seen two of Bannan's gang in the middle of the night walking down the street with ladders. She never thought much about it till the next morning when John noticed they were missing.

I tried to stop John going down to the corner to dig Bannan up. But I couldn't so I had to go with him. He marched up to Bannan's car.

'Where's my ladders, Bannan?'

Bannan just nodded up the close beside the Wire Inn. His men even moved aside to let us through. When we got up the close the ladders were there. Bannan had started an oil drum fire and sat the ladders in it. It was still burning and they had melted down till only seven rungs stuck out above the flames. Molten aluminium ran out the holes in the barrel. It was like a big silver star with a dirty fire burning in the middle. I turned and there was Bannan standing in the close, his legs open like a cowboy film and all his men laughing. The laughing echoed and made me mad. I wanted to grab Bannan and shove his head in the fire. All I remember is screaming and running at him.

When I came to, the close was empty. It was just me and John and the smell of burning ladders. John said Bannan had knocked me out with one punch. But he was still proud of me. At least I stood up for myself. He bought a bottle and took me home. My nose was broke.

CHAPTER SEVEN

Summer was coming to an end and it was all over for the window cleaning run. The ladders were gone. I stayed in for weeks and John went back into his room and closed the blinds. It was even worse when I seen this other window cleaner from Sikeside walking up the street whistling with his ladder on his shoulder.

I was skint. I'd drank the Giro and not even bought any food. I was smoking ashtray douts and drinking tea from a five day tea-bag. I found an old bottle of salad cream in the back of the cupboard and there was an onion with green stalks growing out the top. I was dipping slices of the onion in the cream and thinking up ways to make some money. Then it came to me. There's a farm a mile along the canal. I could go up and see if there's maybe any chicks running loose. Steal one or two. Hope that they're hens and then they can breed with the Red Rooster. I goes up for John.

'Fancy a doss up the canal?'

'The canal?' he goes, giving it the question mark look.

I tell him about my plan. That we might be able to find some chicks running loose and take them home. He shrugs the shoulders and hands me a roll up. All along the canal John makes it clear that he's only going for the walk. Even if we get chicks it doesn't mean he's back on the breeding programme. But that's alright. I'm thinking when I get up and running with the eggs he'll join in and it'll be like nothing ever happened.

But when we get to the farm it's full of cows and pigs. There's not a hen in sight. You'd think a farmer would have even enough hens to get eggs for himself. But no. We head off and no matter how many times I come up with another plan to re-start the chicken run John changes the subject. So we walk along for ages with none of us saying nothing.

'Look!' says John. And there's a field of late tatties as far as the eye could see. He was over the fence first. I pulled two carrier bags from a tree and jumped in and all. If you're ever short of a carrier bag, look up trees. There's always some stuck up there. John pulled the shaws up. The tatties were big and hard. I followed behind him breaking them off and loading them into the carrier bags.

We filled a bag each and headed back home along the old tarmac road. I'm thinking roast tatties and five day tea. When you've nothing, next to nothing is a feast. We lit up a roll up each. I closed my eyes and blew smoke out over the field like a crop duster. Well that's what I'm thinking when up comes this pick-up with a big red face pressed against the glass. It's the Farmer. He spins the pick-up round like the films and stopped on the path in front of us. The door flew open before the thing had stopped. His boot was bumping off the moving gravel. It stops and he jumps out. Up he comes. Chin on chest. Eyes swivelled up at us. Elbows out. He starts ranting.

'Get the tatties over ya pair of ignorant pigs. I sat at my breakfast there and watched yees. The height a cheek howking my produce out my own park.'

He's pointing at the field like a demented referee. Barking mad. You couldn't get a word in edgeways if you wanted to.

'Ah ken yer faces so a dae. Ah ken yer faces and I'll find oot yer names so a will. I'll find oot yer names and it's the Polis for ye – oh aye – the Polis.'

John's not too happy at the mention of polis and he walks away. I follow. And the Farmer follows the two of us. He's so close I can smell his saliva and the reek of cow dung. He snatches John's bag out his hand. There's a split second's stillness. Then John bursts out laughing. I know he's laughing out of nerves but the Farmer doesn't.

'Ya cheeky ignorant pig yee steals my produce and ye've got the lip tae laugh right in my face. Right in my bloody face... whit kind of world we living in for Goads sake? But I ken yer faces and mark my words I'll find oot your names – oh aye – don't think ah won't.'

Then he turned and told the hedges.

'Right in my face he's laughing... wid you credit it?'

By this time I've snuck sideways looking for

somewhere to hide my bag of tatties. He sees them and comes marching at me. But I was thinking, this is my dinner. This is roast tatties and five day tea. He snatched the bag. I snatched the bag back. But then I see a wee bit of fear on his face. I hate that. When you frighten somebody. I hand him the bag and he flings it in the back of his pick-up along with the one he took off John. Then he whips out this knife. A big fold over job. Eight inches anyway.

'John, he's got a knife,' I goes.

Me and John were just about to bolt when the Farmer ran down the hill screaming like an Indian attack. We never knew what was happening. So we hopped the hedge and followed bent over in the field. All the time he's screaming back up to where he thinks we are.

'Ye'll no be getting away ya pair a thieving louts. Ye'll get caught – ye'll hae tae come back for yer caur.'

I looked at John. He looked at me. What car? There's this old sky blue Escort parked squinty halfway down the hill. The Farmer's forcing his knife through the front tyre. It goes down with a loud phutt!

'That'll sort yees oot,' he shouts up, and moves to the next tyre. 'Aye... the polis'll be here when yees come to get yer motor caur. Hee hee hee...'

He let all the tyres down and stormed back up the hill shouting about how that'll teach us. And how the Polis'll be there when we come to get the car back. And if he ever sees us again on his land he'll be well within his rights to blow our heads off with his shotgun that he just wishes he's brung. And in fact he thinks he's got it in the pick-up. And off he goes running towards his pick-up. We ran. Fast. When we got home John took me up and made me my dinner.

CHAPTER EIGHT

By late autumn the Red Rooster was all the man he was ever going to be. Big and gallus. If you went near him he'd have a peck at you. And if he caught you he wouldn't let go. All the weans in Greenend were feart of him. Even the cats and dogs stayed away. Up and down the garden he'd go his head bobbing forwards and backwards. John had been to court for kicking the panels on Bannan's car. He got a deferred sentence. Had to be on good behaviour for six months. His Maw was mortified cos he was in the Advertiser again. She didn't speak to him for three weeks.

This day John was waiting for me at the close as I fed the Red Rooster. We had took to going long walks when we had no money for drink. John decided to go up through the woods and have a look at the new posh houses they've built.

It's hard to believe they've sold houses right next to Greenend but they have. Half of them are lived in now. We've seen them coming and going through Greenend in new cars. All these shiny new people with husbands in suits and kids off the cornflakes advert. They never look at you when they pass. I think they're scared.

The woods are magic. Even if they've took some of them away to build the posh houses. When you're in the middle you could be any-where. There's every colour of leaf. Yellow. Brown. Orange. Even pink. You could be in a fairy-tale. I love sitting under the trees and the smell of mushy ground. There's sometimes birds chirping about criss-crossing the spaces between the trees. We strolled up the hill in silence to Cairnhill house. It sits on the top of the hill like a house out Frankenstein or Dracula.

You couldn't stay away from it. It attracted you. Me and John climbed up the drain pipe and went in. Square beams of light fired through the big dark rooms. Then I got this feeling that some-thing bad was going to happen. I've got the fear and I've got it bad. When we reach the main hall John wants to explore. I want to leave. John takes a look at the fear on my face and out we go. When I drop from the window I breathe in big gasps of air and light.

We head into the new houses. It's like walking onto a film set. It's amazing how completely different kinds of people can live so close. It's all polished cars and the smell of different wives' cooking. Me and John's right out of place walking up the street and everybody's looking at us. They know we're from Greenend. It's wrote all over us. Our walk. Our gear. The run-down look on our faces.

'C'mon John,' I go, 'everybody's looking at us.'

But he's not leaving.

'It's a free country,' he says.

And we get deeper and deeper into the scheme. We walk through the scents of different women passing with prams. They're like models out a catalogue. The kind of women we can only dream about.

Across the road four of them are talking and nodding over. I'm getting hot and bothered now even though it's a cold day in late October. They think we're up to no good. I can see why they're bothered. Doors lying open. Good clothes on the washing line. Bikes on their own. Faces are watching from dark windows. Eyes are peering through hedges and from behind washing lines. Somebody's probably phoned the Polis already.

'Eh excuse me there are two chaps walking about our estate – and they seems rather – well rough if you know what I mean. They're acting very suspiciously and I suspect they're planning a job. I've written a description!'

Up ahead this skip lies half on the pavement, half on the road. At the very edge of the scheme.

'Yo ho – Skip ahoy!' says John. He loves a good skip.

Skips are usually full of goodies in posh areas. John's got a theory about that. He thinks they throw good stuff out to show their neighbours how rich they are. Mrs McGinty throws out a half decent three piece suite so Mrs McGonigle chucks a couple of beds and a wardrobe. McGinty hears about the bed, rips out the kitchen just fitted a year ago, and skips it. McGonigle responds with her kitchen cooker and fridge. On and on they go till they've got to buy stuff out of Comet to throw out.

We walk by the skip slow, looking over the edge. It looks like all plasterboard and old timbers when something glints. I scan the street. Nobody watching. I harden the belly muscles and balance into the skip. There's a wire. I tug and on the end is a silver toaster. Morphy Richards. I hand it to John and he dusts it as I'm getting out the skip.

That's when the polis arrived. Butsy and the guy with red hair again. They shoved us in the back of the van. John still had the toaster. As they drove us out of the posh scheme it seemed like there was lines of women on the streets with folded arms watching us. John said they probably expected a war with the Greenenders and this was the first battle. Butsy stopped the van on the edge of the woods and asked John what was going on. John said we were only out a walk and we seen this skip. He went quiet then burst out greeting.

'Don't lift me, eh no – Butsy. My Maw'll fling me out for sure this time.'

Butsy and the other polis had a wee talk. They asked to see the toaster. It's a wreck to them. Covered in dust and dented. They let us go with a warning never to go near that scheme again. John thanked Butsy and off we went in through the trees. Back towards Greenend. I never said nothing to John about the crying.

When we got to the wee burn I dipped the corner of my donkey jacket in and cleaned the toaster. I was well pleased that it had a Thickness Setting. It could do outsiders. I always wanted one of them. The more I cleaned it the more I learned. You could set it light brown to totally burnt. It was the best toaster I had ever seen.

We went home and John said he'd not be out for a couple of days. He went up the stairs and next thing I seen the blinds closing. Even though I knew he was depressed and I should've tried to do something about it, I never. I couldn't stop thinking about my new toaster. Couldn't wait to get in and try it out.

I plugged it in and switched on the plug with a stick cos the toaster was wet still. Nothing happened. I changed the fuse. Nothing. I screwed the side off with a knife. The element was broke in the middle. I twisted the two ends together and screwed the sides back on. I switched it on and it started glowing and hissing.

I tried inviting John down for a slice of toast

but he was on a downer. He said it was a sad day when you couldn't walk up streets in your own town. Would we get them lifted if they walked through Greenend?

'It's only a daft posh scheme John,' I said. 'Don't let it get you down.'

But there was lot more than that bothering him.

'I can't walk up there or I get lifted, and I can't walk here cos of Bannan. What's the point in even going out the door?'

I knew not to try to persuade him. He was on a downward spiral and all I could do was wait till he started to come up again.

CHAPTER NINE

By December John was room bound. He was on the sick and didn't even have to go out to sign on. The Doctor was giving him all these different pills but they weren't working. He had a Monday Book and his Maw cashed it for him. His was probably the only Monday Book in Greenend that Bannan didn't have a say in.

Christmas came and went and I never seen him except on a Friday when I'd visit him with a bottle and some cans. He'd pay for them one week. I'd pay for them the next. By February I thought there was no hope for him. That he'd never come out of that room. The Doctor was saying they might have to take him into Ward 24. But they were going to try these new pills on him first. Prozac they were called.

The snow was tumbling down this morning at

the start of March. I was staring out the window watching it fall. The Red Rooster was huddled in beside the wrecked shed. I had food and fags and was settling in for a few days bad weather. Then the door goes.

I was surprised to see John. And he's smiling. He barges past me waving the Advertiser.

'Wait till you see this,' he goes.

And he lays the paper out on the floor. We crouch down and he points to a wee advert. Blue Hen – three pounds. Apply Headrigg Farm Plains. I took in a big happy breath! John was back on the breeding programme. The new pills must be working. And we had the top dog male out there ready to go to town. And! And this is important!! And! We know this one's going to be a hen!

Plains is six miles from Greenend. Six there and six back. I chipped in two quid and John chipped in a quid he stole out his Maw's purse. And just to show me he was serious he brung a bulb down. He hands me it.

'Spare,' is all he says.

I put it in my toilet and he waited in the close. We had to act fast. There's no telling that a Blue Hen won't get snapped up.

It was freezing. One of them days when your shoulders rub off your ears. Our words were muffled by the fog they came out in. On the corner everything was arranged around Bannan. Like he's the hub of a wheel. Power. That's what it was. A few of the boys looked over. Some nodded but Bannan was staring us out.

'Don't look,' says John. 'Keep walking.'

Bannan shouted a few things but we kept going. Once we cleared the corner I felt at ease. And so did John cos his head came back up out of his jacket. We strode out towards Plains. The snowflakes were coming down like miniature saw-blades. They were cutting into our skin. But that's nothing. With a wee bit of imagination you can think yourself back into the Klondike at the furnace. Me and John and big Bannan, when there was hardly a bad bone in his body, having a laugh and a couple of cans. Then the snow biting your face becomes furnace heat. That cheered me up and I imagined a year from now; hutches all over the garden and me and John out with trays collecting eggs. Selling them round Greenend. All these boiled eggs and omelettes rushed back into my head. I glanced at John and his thoughts were the same. We smiled. I mind the exact moment John smiled a wee snowflake landed on the end of his nose and he licked it off. Going cross eyed at the same time. And we laughed. And he put his arm round me and gave me a wee hug. And I gave him one back. It was the happiest time of my life. We smiled on through the thickening snow. Two lights in the darkness of March.

When we got to Plains we paid three quid to a thirteen year old laddie. We told him all about our bad luck and our new breeding plans. He gave us a couple of tips and wished us all the best. The walk down the road was a lot quicker. A new snowfall had took the sting out the air and we kept swapping the Blue Hen. I'd have her up my jumper for a mile then John'd have her up his. Taking turns at being pregnant with the future. The whole world was that warm hen. I love the way snow affects sound. It was like beyond me and John and the Blue Hen nothing existed. The place was white and our footprints behind were driving us into the promise of uncharted lands of snow.

CHAPTER TEN

We were back at the corner in no time. Bannan was strutting about giving orders.

'Cross over,' John said.

We crossed over. But Bannan seen us.

'Hey what's that you've got!' he shouts.

'Ignore him,' John says.

We marched faster. Bannan kept on shouting. 'Stop!'

We kept going. Out the side of my eye I could see Bannan struggling in his jacket for something. Some of the corner boys were scattering. Others grinned.

'Stop!'

Bannan had a gun.

'John – he's got a gun!'

But John pressed the Blue Hen into his belly.

'Keep going,' John said.

'This is your last chance!' shouts Bannan.

That was the moment I seen what dignity was. It was John. It was the Blue Hen up his jook. The palms of his hands pressing her soft feathers. Dignity was John keeping on walking with that gun pointing.

The shot rang out the exact same time as this groove made its way under the snow. A line like a pipe appeared between me and John. A pipe of snow bursting open at the seam. And a starbrust of slush exploded at the kerb. I could feel the corner boys walking away from Bannan. I turned a bit as we walked. John never even broke his stride. Bannan pointed the gun again.

'John – I'm telling you – Stop!' he shouted.

We turned the corner as the shot went off.

When we walked into the back garden John was shaking. That's when I realized so was I. We never said nothing about the gun. It was like it never happened. The Red Rooster swung its head round but it stood well back. By this time it was pretty adept at getting up onto the roof and that's where it went. There wasn't another bird up there. We put the Blue Hen in the hutch and watched. But the Red Rooster stayed on the roof. Out waited us. Watching. Glaring. We decided it was as shy as we'd be if somebody brought us home a woman to marry. It might be bold and tough but, as John pointed out, it was still a virgin and that's why it was bashful. Probably be alright in the morning.

I woke up the next morning about eight with this racket. A squawking like I've never heard. I ran out the back and there's John and he's just pulled the head off the Red Rooster.

Murdering bastard! Murdering bastard! he's shouting.

The claws of the Red Rooster are still twitching but the blood's spurting out its neck. Onto John's hands. Dripping into the snow. I look in the hutch and there's the Blue Hen lying stiff and dead beneath the ghostly daylight glow of the hundred watt bulb. Both her eyes are pecked out.

Also in the Vista Series:

THE CHERRY SUNDAE COMPANY
by Isla Dewar

You have to bide your time when you live a life
of crime. You have to wait for the moment.
Tina and me discovered that when we founded
The Cherry Sundae Company. Not that we
thought that what we were doing was really
against the law. We were just
balancing things up a bit.

It seemed to us that there was only so much
money in the world and some people had too
much of it. Others hadn't enough. It was our
aim to sort that out. You could say that we were
vigilantes. Of course it all went horribly wrong.
But then, everything that Tina and me
do always does.

Isla Dewar worked as a journalist before
turning to books. She lives in Fife with her
husband, Bob, a cartoonist and illustrator.
She has two sons.

THE WHITE CLIFFS
by Suhayl Saadi

Adam and Lily meet in a little seaside café in winter. It's bleak and lonely, and they're both looking for love. Far out at sea, they can see a dark shape that moves and shifts. It looks like an island – but no one else seems to know what it is. In fact, no one else admits to seeing it.

Adam is a writer who isn't writing anything; Lily is a waitress who says she is French. But nothing is what it seems. When they reach the island it's not black but white. And white cliffs rise above them. Beneath them, the sea itself, lie the ghosts of the past.

Suhayl Saadi is an award-winning Glasgow-based writer. His work has been published internationally, and also broadcast on BBC Radio. *The Burning Mirror* (Polygon), a short story collection, was short-listed for the Saltire First Book Prize in 2001. He has also written a radio play, *The Dark Island* (BBC Radio 4), and a novel, *Psychoraag,* (Black and White Publishing), both appearing in 2004.
www.suhaylsaadi.com

Moira Forsyth, *Series Editor for the Sandstone Vistas, writes:*

The Sandstone Vista Series of novellas has been developed for readers who are not used to reading full length novels, or for those who simply want to enjoy a 'quick read' which is satisfying and well written.